DAVID O. MCKAY LIBRARY

3 1404 00716 3717

ZOOLUTIONS

D0796715

APR 0 2002

WITHDRAWN

FEB 1 4 2023

DAVID O. McKAY LIBRARY
BYU-IDAHO

PROPERT
DAVID O. McKAY LIBRARY
BYU-IDAHO
REXBURG ID 83460-0405

SCHOOL LIBRARY MEDIA SERIES
Edited by Diane de Cordova Biesel

ZOOLUTIONS

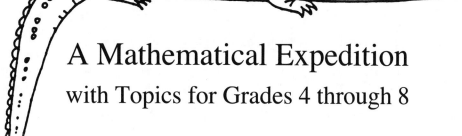

A Mathematical Expedition
with Topics for Grades 4 through 8

by
Anne Burgunder
Vaunda Nelson

School Library Media Series, No. 6

The Scarecrow Press, Inc.
Lanham, Md., & London

SCARECROW PRESS, INC.

Published in the United States of America
by Scarecrow Press, Inc.
4720 Boston Way
Landam, Maryland 20706

4 Pleydell Gardens, Folkestone
Kent CT20 2DN, England

Copyright © 1993, 1996 by Anne Stanko Burgunder and Vaunda Micheaux Nelson

Cover art by Scott Deutsch
Thanks to: Drew Nelson, Elaine Olds, Judy Thoft, and Shady Side Academy

The purchase of this book entitles an individual teacher to reproduce pages for use in a single classroom. Reproduction for use in an entire school building or system is prohibited.

Zoolutions originally appeared in article form as "Math Safari" in *Learning Magazine* in August 1992.

British Cataloguing-in-Publication Information Available

Library of Congress Cataloging-in-Publication Data

Burgunder, Anne, 1965–
Zoolutions : a mathematical expedition with topics for grades 4 through 8 /
by Anne Burgunder and Vaunda Nelson
p.   cm — (School library media series ; no. 6)
1. Mathematics—Study and teaching (Elementary).   I. Nelson, Vaunda Micheaux.
II. Title. III. Series.
QA135.5B836   1996   372.7'044—dc20   95-25206   CIP

ISBN 0-8108-3075-2 (cloth : alk. paper)

⊗ ™The paper used in this publication meets the minimum requirements of
American National Standard for Information Sciences—Permanence of
Paper for Printed Library Materials, ANSI Z39.48–1984.
Manufactured in the United States of America.

CONTENTS

Editor's Foreword

The School Library Media Series is directed to the school library media specialist, particularly the building level librarian. The multifaceted role of the librarian as educator, collection developer, curriculum developer, and information specialist is examined. The series includes concise, practical books on topical and current subjects related to programs and services.

Combining mathematics and research, *Zoolutions: A Mathematical Expedition* will lead students to explore many avenues of adventure with animals. Burgunder and Nelson have gone beyond drill and practice toward the life skills of cooperative learning and problem solving. The activities are so intriguing that they will help students *want* to learn.

This project was chosen by the Association for Library Service to Children, one of the divisions of the American Library Association, to receive the 1994 Econo-Clad Literature Program Award.

Diane de Cordova Biesel
Series Editor

WHAT IS ZOOLUTIONS?

- It's a mathematical, scientific, geographic, informational adventure.

- It's solving problems as members of cooperative groups.

- It's reading critically and analyzing information.

- It's thinking purposefully and acquiring competence in mathematics and research.

- It's a journey toward bringing research skills, mathematical knowledge and deductive reasoning into everyday life.

Zoolutions is a team-taught interdisciplinary program which takes place in the school library and uses the study of animals as a basis for problem solving.

WHAT ARE THE GOALS OF THE PROGRAM?

- To enable students to recognize that there is a real-world need for each math skill by providing them with reasons for wanting to learn the various operations.

- To enable students to see the library not as a "special subject," but as a resource for all content areas.

- To provide students experiences with numbers beyond drill and practice.

- To show students that factual information can be found in fiction sources.

- To enable students to make connections between the knowledge they have already acquired and new areas of information.

- To build a community in which librarians and classroom teachers, children, and their classmates work together.

- To cultivate the natural curiosity that young children have, to lead students to ask themselves, "If this is true, I wonder if . . .?"

- To enable students to make connections between the information they receive from the external world and their internal lives.

- To help students acquire skills that will put them in a position to better control their own learning in and beyond their lives in the classroom.

- To enable students to recognize the value of information and the power that comes with knowing how to find it.

- To meet the goals recommended by the National Council of Teachers of Mathematics' *Curriculum and Evaluation Standards,* * and to provide an environment in which mathematical power will be realized.

*National Council of Teachers of Mathematics. *Curriculum and Evaluation Standards for School Mathematics*. Reston, VA.: NCTM, 1989.

WHAT ARE THE CURRICULAR BENEFITS OF ZOOLUTIONS?

Zoolutions conforms to the objectives for library media programs as stated in *Information Power: Guidelines for School Library Media Specialists,* prepared by the American Association of School Librarians and the Association for Educational Communications and Technology.

The Zoolutions program strengthens the library's position as a central part of school life by integrating research skills into the curriculum. It contributes to lifelong learning by cultivating problem-solving skills and stimulating an interest in using information and ideas. It also encourages partnerships between library media specialists, teachers, students, and administrators—partnerships which are necessary to the success of interdisciplinary education.

As schools begin to address current needs for math reform recommended by the National Council of Teachers of Mathematics, the roles and expectations of both teachers and students are beginning to change.

> Woven into the fabric of the *Professional Standards for Teaching Mathematics* are five major shifts in the environment of mathematics classrooms that are needed to move from current practice to mathematics teaching for the empowerment of students. We need to shift—
>
>   — **toward** classrooms as mathematical communities—**away from** classrooms as simply a collection of individuals;
>
>   — **toward** logic and mathematical evidence as verification—**away from** the teacher as the sole authority for right answers;
>
>   — **toward** mathematical reasoning—**away from** merely memorizing procedures;
>
>   — **toward** conjecturing, inventing, and problem solving—**away from** an emphasis on mechanistic answer-finding;
>
>   — **toward** connecting mathematics, its ideas, and its applications—**away from** treating mathematics as a body of isolated concepts and procedures.

Professional Standards for Teaching Mathematics
National Council of Teachers of Mathematics, March 1991,
page 3.

WHY ANIMALS?

Most children are interested in animals, and resource materials for animal subjects are abundant. Exploring questions about animals dissolves the belief that math is only a set of rules to be memorized and that these rules will have little use outside of the classroom. Animal topics offer the opportunity to branch out in many directions, and problems that address all areas of curricular math standards can be devised. Solutions to Zoolutions questions represent something meaningful, providing another piece of the puzzle in the students' understanding of the world around them, of environmental issues, and of their place in the natural world.

HOW ARE STUDENTS PREPARED FOR ZOOLUTIONS?

Because most students are accustomed to working independently, they often lack the skills required to work successfully on group projects. So, prior to beginning Zoolutions, and throughout its duration, teachers define, model and discuss cooperative behaviors with their students.

In addition, before starting the program, students are introduced to library resources including: almanacs, encyclopedias, dictionaries, the *Guinness Book of World Records,* atlases, the card catalog, and indexes such as *Children's Magazine Guide*.

There are a variety of ways to teach students library skills. In the best methods, classroom teachers accompany their students to the library where the children are provided with hands-on activities which send them directly to the card or on-line catalog, to the shelves, and to specific reference books. Scavenger hunts, for instance, are fun incentives for getting students to use resources. With practice, guidance, and support from the librarian and classroom teachers, children will gain confidence in their abilities to find information.

HOW IS THE PROGRAM IMPLEMENTED?

Upon beginning Zoolutions, student explorers are organized into groups of three or four. (NOTE: Cooperative groups work best when diversity is maximized. A student who isn't strong in math may be a great reader. Students learn to build on the strengths of each group member.)

Each Zoolutions group receives a different animal topic to investigate. Varying the topics eliminates resource overlap and potential conflicts between groups, and can allow the students to choose a topic according to interest, length or complexity. (NOTE: Teachers may wish to assign topics according to their sense of each particular group's need for challenge.)

All groups receive a general list of Zoolutions supplies that they may need on their quests (see **Appendix A**). Supplies include a card or on-line catalog, an atlas, an almanac, a dictionary, encyclopedias, *Children's Magazine Guide, National Geographic Index,* and a few specific resources used for some of the beginning topics. As on an expedition, readily available supplies dwindle and the explorers must rely more and more upon their own instincts and their survival (research) skills.

Students should read the entire topic before beginning. Questions may be stated toward the end of the topic that students should be thinking about throughout their research.

The Zoolutions process requires that students:

1. locate information concerning a given animal;

2. read and analyze this information; and

3. determine how to solve each problem, using math and/or reasoning.

Students are expected to record all math strategies and the resources used for each solution. All members work together to agree on each answer before moving on.

WHAT ARE THE TEACHERS' ROLES IN THE ZOOLUTIONS PROCESS?

The primary role of the teacher in Zoolutions is as a facilitator. Within this role teachers will:

1. **encourage students.**

   Zoolutions is not a race. If teachers continually stress that the *process* is as important as arriving at a *correct solution,* students are less likely to become anxious when a particular problem takes considerable time and effort.

2. **observe and monitor the group process.**

   Information gathered during these observations can be useful in communicating students' strengths and weaknesses as members of cooperative groups and as individuals. For a checklist of cooperative behaviors, see **Appendix B**.

3. **ask questions to stimulate or direct group thinking.**

   On some Zoolutions questions teachers may be tempted to define a term for students, especially if they ask. Don't give in to this impulse. Often the children are asked questions which *they* need to analyze, discuss and define for themselves. Confusion offers a unique opportunity for learning. When the gap between ambiguity and knowing is great, the desire for resolution magnifies. When the pieces of the puzzle come together, understanding becomes absolute.

4. **help students examine their research strategies.**

   Students who experience frustration in locating information usually need only be directed to retrace their steps. Referring group members back to their Zoolutions supplies list can help them consider where they've already been in their search, and where they might go next. Do not locate and/or pull resources for students. The Zoolutions process requires that they locate information for themselves.

5. **teach a specific math operation or how to use a particular resource when the students have a desire or need to know.**

   Students who haven't yet learned long division often recognize the need to divide, and they will want someone to teach them. Teaching methods may include manipulatives, pictures and diagrams, calculators, and pencil and paper algorithms.

6. **interview students.** (See section on assessment.)

HOW ARE STUDENTS ASSESSED?

1. **Through cooperative behavior check lists.**

   After each Zoolutions session, students are expected to evaluate their abilities to work cooperatively. One step in this evaluation process is the completion of a group check list (see **Appendix B**). Behaviors included on this list focus on growth and development issues frequently addressed in the overall assessment of elementary school students.

2. **Through writing.**

   Students are required to reflect on their Zoolutions experience in their learning logs. This reflection can be stimulated by posing questions to the students, such as: "What did your group do well today?" "What would you like to see your group do better next time?" "Choose one question you worked on today and tell how you went about solving it and what obstacles, if any, you encountered."

   Through writing, students can discover what they know and understand, as well as what they may want or need to know more about. By reading student writing (see **Appendix C**), educators can discover each child's strengths and tailor the learning environment to better meet the needs of individuals.

3. **Through interviews.**

   After a group has completed a Zoolutions topic, the participants hold a conference to review their work and prepare for an interview. Group members use this conference time to discuss their topic, understanding that they will be required to explain (without using numbers) how each solution was achieved. For example, in responding to a question regarding the length of an elephant's tusk, one student said: "According to the author of *Elephants, Wildlife at Risk,* an elephant's tusk is 6.7 inches for each year that an elephant is alive. If an elephant is two years old, the tusk will be 13.4 inches long. If an elephant is three years old, the tusk will be 20.1 inches." In explaining the process without using numbers, the student went on to say, "In other words, to find out how long an elephant's tusk is, we multiply how old an elephant is by the number of inches the tusk grows per year."

Interviews are conducted by one member of the teaching team, while other student groups continue their work under the supervision of the second team member.

During the interview, students are called upon at random to respond to questions and share what they have learned. Careful questioning can lead students to offer more information than was required of them by the topic. When students' natural inquisitiveness entices them beyond what has been asked, they take the first steps toward directing their own learning. Later they may want to develop their own topics.

At Shady Side Academy Junior School, points earned for correct processes and answers were exchanged for "timbala" (Zoolutions currency) which were accumulated and used for participation in an animal adoption (care and maintenance) program at the local zoo.

Since each group's processes cannot be predicted, and educator goals may vary, teaching teams are free to develop their own standards for payment, just as they are free to be creative in determining another meaningful exchange for earned "timbala." Whatever teachers decide, equal emphasis should be placed upon processes and solutions. Adding or deducting timbala for positive or negative cooperative behavior evaluations can provide incentive for improving and/or maintaining cooperative skills (see **Appendix D** for "timbala").

WHERE ARE THE ANSWERS?

Implicit in the Zoolutions process is the journey, a journey in which the destination is less important than the method of getting there. Answers are secondary to process. Therefore, we have chosen not to provide specific answers for each question. As in real-world problem solving, teachers will receive a range of answers from students, depending upon what resources are used and who is interpreting the information.

Providing answer keys assumes that everyone has the same resources available, that all sources contain the same kind of information, and that all information is consistent. Answer keys also assume that information from only one source will be used to solve a given problem. For instance, when specific statistical information is required to solve a question, teachers should encourage students to check more than one resource, compare information, discuss why this information may vary, and decide as a group what statistics they should use. In addition, group dynamics will vary, as will methods of solving problems because individual thought processes differ.

As Marilyn Burns says:

> In real-life problems, you're rarely given all the information you need in one tidy package; you often have to collect the data and often from a variety of sources. There's rarely only one possible method or strategy that emerges from real-life problems; usually you choose one from several viable possibilities. You don't always know for sure if the solution you choose is the "right" or "best" one; you decide on one plausible solution and it may be only later that you can evaluate your choice. Sometimes you never find out for sure; life has no answer book.

> Burns, Marilyn. *About Teaching Mathematics: A K-8 Resource*. Sausalito, CA: © 1992 Math Solutions Publications. p. 15. Reprinted with permission.

In order for teachers to fully understand and appreciate Zoolutions, they will want to experience the process of solving the problems in their own libraries, using their own resources.

Lists of specific and general sources used in developing these topics have been provided. These lists are for teachers' use only so that they can determine whether their library collections include the kinds of resources they may need. If a library does not house a particular resource, it should not be assumed that a topic or question cannot be used. Each school's library collection may include alternate resources that will provide comparable or perhaps better information.

HOW LONG WILL ZOOLUTIONS TAKE?

Zoolutions is ideal for use during flexible scheduling times. Teachers need not worry about fitting the project into a limited time frame, or rushing students to complete a given number of topics. Students may spend an entire Zoolutions session reading and discussing what they've read, or searching for information. A group may work on one question for a whole period or more, or finish five or six questions. It is important to provide students with time to thoroughly work through the process. Math need not be done every Zoolutions period. Additional math instruction should take place at other times during the week.

Best results are achieved when students can spend 40-60 minutes in the library two to three times a week over an eight-to-twelve-week period. (NOTE: Educators who may not have the luxury of flexible schedules will have to work within their own time constraints.) When total time allocated for the Zoolutions project runs out, students should end the topics where they are, then be interviewed about the questions which they have completed. Many students may desire to finish uncompleted topics on their own.

HOW DO I DEVELOP MY OWN TOPICS?

Current educational reform mandates a move away from teacher-directed environments to instructional settings which are more student centered. In order to do this, teachers are learning to listen to students and follow their leads in developing curriculum.

When creating topics for Zoolutions, teachers need not feel they have to ask all the questions. Students of all ages want to know about animals. In an atmosphere where children feel free to ask questions and explore, topics can begin to materialize as students' natural inquisitiveness takes them in many directions. Elaine Olds, a teacher at Shady Side Academy, experienced the process in this way:

> My first grade class had been discussing tigers in preparation for a school-wide presentation featuring the signs of the Chinese calendar, and I wondered if the students could suggest a way to integrate math into the unit. I asked them what kinds of math questions they could pose about tigers.
>
> The first responses sounded just like story problems from the pages of a math workbook. "If there were two tigers and then another two tigers came, how many tigers would there be?" That was not a question about tigers, it was about two plus two. I mentioned this to the students and asked them to try again. "What do you want to find out about tigers that has to do with math?"
>
> "How many whiskers do tigers have?" "How long is a tiger's tail? How long are a tiger's whiskers?" "If you laid the whiskers end to end, how far would they reach?" "How big is the biggest tiger?" "How many boys would it take to be as big as the biggest tiger?"
>
> I filled two pages with the questions that followed one after another. As I wrote, I responded with questions of my own. "What would you need to know before you could answer the question about how many boys it would take to weigh as much as the biggest tiger?" They understood immediately that they would need to decide whether biggest meant heaviest, longest, or tallest and to also determine the size or weight of both the tiger and the boy.
>
> "If you really want to find out the answers to some of these questions, I think perhaps we need to do some research," I suggested. Research is an impressive word to six and seven year old children.

I had no idea if the answers to all of the questions generated by the class could be found in the books that were available to us. It seems to me that if we are truly teaching children to be comfortable about problem solving in real-life situations, we have to be honest about the fact that the answers we seek are not always readily available.

We never did find out the length of a tiger's whiskers, but once the students began reading, they made many interesting discoveries that led to new questions. One boy learned that a male tiger can weigh as much as 500 pounds, but that the weight of females seldom exceeded 350. They began to notice the weights of some of the world's other large animals, such as the world's largest turtle, at 1,600 pounds. "I wonder how many tigers it would take to weigh as much as that turtle," one child asked, and another chimed in, "I wonder how many tigers it would take to weigh as much as a blue whale!"

The children were eager to find answers and solutions to the questions and problems they had posed about tigers. Soon they were picking up books and articles that were beyond their usual reading levels, and they explored math concepts not usually part of a first grade curriculum. The students were enthusiastic throughout the entire process, because they had taken a topic and made it their own.

Unfortunately, the opportunity to involve students in the creation of Zoo-lutions topics doesn't always exist. At such times, teachers can tap into their own curiosity and consider the kinds of questions children might ask. Topics also can develop from springboards such as these:

How tall is the animal? How much does it weigh?

How much does it eat in a day, a week, a year, a lifetime?

How long does it live in captivity, in the wild?

What is its size at birth? How fast does it grow?

How long is the gestation period?

How long does a newborn stay with its mother?

When does it first begin to walk, see, hunt, etc.?

How many in a litter?

How fast can it go?

How long does it take it to travel _____miles?

What is the largest, fastest, oldest, etc., ever recorded? How long ago was this record set?

How long does it take them to _____?

How far can they swim from shore, be heard, etc.?

How many live in a given area?

How does it compare with other species?

Is the population growing or decreasing? At what rate?

How many are estimated to be in existence, and what percent of these have actually been sighted?

Where do they live longer—in captivity or in the wild? How much longer?

How long do scientists believe they have existed?

When was the first captive one brought to the U.S.?

How far was it transported?

How does information appearing in a particular fiction book com-pare with factual information?

How do statistics about this animal compare to you?

Math conversions—feet to miles, minutes to hours, ounces to pounds, etc.

Hypothetical questions, such as, "If ___ then ___?"

FINAL WORDS FROM THE AUTHORS

Zoolutions is the result of collaboration between a classroom teacher and a school librarian. It would not have been born without both of us. Nor could the project have been developed without a flexible school administration that encouraged its staff to be creative and to take risks. Cooperation and support from teaching colleagues also played an important role in helping to push the project forward. We wish to thank the administration and staff of Shady Side Academy in Pittsburgh for this foundation.

We began developing and implementing Zoolutions at the Academy's Junior School in 1989. Our initial plan was to integrate mathematics and library skills, but, once seed met water, the project took on a life of its own and blossomed into a much broader interdisciplinary program. Much of the early process was based on a leap of faith involving trial and error, instinct, and the belief that what we were doing would lead to something more meaningful than even we knew at the time.

In many ways, Zoolutions continues to be a kind of living organism, always growing and evolving. Often, we don't know whether a question will work—how children will interpret or respond to it—until we've tried it. New ideas for questions, topics, and methods regularly come our way through student input, new print resources, and out-of-school influences such as programs on PBS or the Discovery Channel on a Saturday afternoon.

We encourage teachers and librarians who implement Zoolutions at their schools also to view the project as a living organism, one that will evolve and shape itself according to the environment in which it exists. Those who wish to deviate from the map we have drawn are encouraged do so. Be daring, explore, and enjoy the journey.

ZOOLUTIONS TOPICS

The topics included in this book were designed for fourth-through eighth-grade students. However, Zoolutions can easily be adapted for use with younger students. (See "How Do I Develop My Own Topics?")

In learning mathematics, students need to be immersed in a variety of problem-solving situations which expose them to the use of all operations. Therefore, no one topic is devoted to the practice of a single mathematical operation, and mathematical operations are not presented in a traditional sequence (i.e., addition first, then subtraction, etc.). Students may be required to add, subtract, multiply, and divide using whole numbers, decimals, and fractions within the same topic.

Because no two Zoolutions groups work on the same topic at the same time, topics will not be used in any specific order. The first five or six topics, however, offer the least overall complexity. Each topic presents a different challenge which may involve the use of an unfamiliar resource, a new problem-solving approach, or the amount or complexity of reading required.

RESOURCES AND MATERIALS

Bibliographies at the end of each topic include only resources that were available in our school library at the time the topics were developed. Therefore, some materials are more current than others. Each school's library collection will vary and may include alternate resources that will provide comparable or perhaps better information. Educators should keep in mind that some entries in *The Guinness Book of World Records* appear one year and are omitted the next. It should not be assumed that the most current source is always the best. Back issues of magazines and/or copies of articles may be available through public libraries, on-line services, or directly from specific publishers.

MICE

1. Estimate the number of mice the illustrator had to draw in *The Church Mouse* by Graham Oakley. How did you get your answer?

_____

_____

_____

_____

_____

Approximately how many mice per page is this?

_____

_____

_____

_____

2. Locate the part of the story that reads: "The parson says if we do a few odd jobs we'll be paid in cheese, best quality. . . A vote was taken on what kinds of cheese the parson should buy, and the result was: . . ."*

Read on and write down the number of mice that voted for each kind of cheese.

_____

_____

_____

_____

*Reprinted with the permission of Atheneum Books for Young Readers, an imprint of Simon & Schuster Children's Publishing Division from THE CHURCH MOUSE by Graham Oakley. Coyright © 1972 Graham Oakley.

How many mice voted in all?

_____

_____

_____

_____

3. What is the difference between the number of types of cheese selected by the mouse voters and the total number of named cheeses?

_____

_____

_____

_____

_____

4. How old must a person be to vote in the United States?

_____

_____

_____

_____

_____

5. Of the mice that voted in *The Church Mouse*, how many were said to be underage?

_____

_____

_____

_____

_____

6. How many votes counted? Explain your answer.

_____

_____

_____

_____

_____

7. If the mice could be paid in 97.5 pounds of Cheddar, 85.25 pounds of Cheshire, or 116 pounds of Wensleydale, which would be their best choice? Which cheese should they choose second? Explain your answers.

_____

_____

_____

_____

_____

8. If Cheddar cheese costs $1.21 per pound and Wensleydale costs $.95 per pound, which would be less expensive for the mice if they received the number of pounds given in Question 7? How much cheaper would it be?

_____

_____

_____

_____

_____

9. If there was a sale and Cheddar cheese was 40% off and Wensley-dale was 50% off, how much per pound would each cheese cost?

_____

_____

_____

_____

_____

10. How much would the mice pay for 97.5 pounds of Cheddar cheese on sale?

_____

_____

_____

_____

_____

11. How much would they pay for 116 pounds of Wensleydale on sale?

_____

_____

_____

_____

12. If each mouse eats 1/4 pound of cheese per week, how much cheese would all the voting mice eat in a week?

_____

_____

_____

_____

_____

How long would the largest cheese ever made last them?

_____

_____

_____

_____

13. If Sampson, the church cat and reformed mouser, had a change of heart and decided to go for the world record, at three mice per day how long would it take him to catch the number of mice you estimated in Question 1?

_____

_____

_____

_____

14. If Sampson lived to be 20 years old and caught three mice per day, would he be the champion mouser? If not, who holds the record for mousing?

_____

_____

_____

_____

_____

MICE
Bibliography

The Guinness Book of World Records. New York: Facts on File, 1991.

Oakley, Graham. *The Church Mouse.* New York: MacMillan Publishing Co., 1972.

The World Almanac and Book of Facts. New York: World Almanac, 1992.

The World Book Encyclopedia. Chicago: World Book, Inc., 1990.

GREAT LAKES FISH

1. In a 1989 wildlife magazine article about Great Lakes fish, approximately how many pounds of fat trout and salmon does Jim Truchan catch each summer?

_____

_____

_____

_____

_____

2. If Truchan was fishing for a family of four, and 20 pounds of fish would feed them for two weeks, how many weeks worth of food did Truchan catch each summer?

_____

_____

_____

_____

_____

3. Based on your answer to Question 2, and on what you've learned from reading the 1989 article, should Truchan consider giving any fish to his friends? Explain.

_____

_____

_____

_____

4. Since the date of Truchan's birth, how much money did Canada and the United States spend on purifying the Great Lakes' waters?

_____

_____

_____

_____

_____

5. If Canada and the United States contributed equal amounts of money, how much did each spend?

_____

_____

_____

_____

_____

6. How much would the United States have contributed per year since the date of Truchan's birth?

_____

_____

_____

_____

7. According to a 1989 *National Geographic* article entitled "Great Lakes Pollution: Still Dangerous," how many times higher is the risk of cancer after eating 11 servings of large Lake Michigan trout than is minimally acceptable by the Environmental Protection Agency?

_____

_____

_____

_____

8. How many people get their drinking water from the Great Lakes?

_____

_____

_____

_____

9. How many people live around the Great Lakes?

_____

_____

_____

_____

10. How many people living around the Great Lakes do not get their drinking water from them?

_____

_____

_____

_____

Why do you think this is so?

_____

_____

_____

_____

From what other sources might these people get their drinking
water?

_____

_____

_____

_____

GREAT LAKES FISH
Bibliography

"Great Lakes Pollution: Still Dangerous." *National Geographic,* Dec. 1989, Geographica section.

Schmidt, Wayne A. "Are Great Lakes Fish Safe to Eat?" *National Wildlife,* Aug./Sept. 1989, pp. 16-19.

DOMESTIC CATS

1. In the beginning of a book about a domestic cat written by Mary Stolz, a litter of kittens is born. How many kittens were in the litter?

_____

_____

_____

_____

_____

2. What is a litter?

_____

_____

_____

_____

_____

3. On average, how many kittens are in the litter of a domestic cat?

_____

_____

_____

_____

_____

4. How many kittens were there in the largest litter of domestic kittens ever recorded?

_____

_____

_____

_____

_____

5. What is the difference between the number of kittens in the average litter and in the largest litter?

_____

_____

_____

_____

_____

6. *Exactly* how long ago was the largest litter of domestic cats born? (Do not round off your answer to the number of years only; include the number of months and days.)

_____

_____

_____

_____

_____

7. How many kittens in the largest litter were stillborn?

_____

_____

_____

_____

_____

8. What does stillborn mean?

_____

_____

_____

_____

_____

9. How many kittens in the largest litter survived?

_____

_____

_____

_____

How many of the surviving kittens were female?

_____

_____

_____

_____

10. What is the gestation period for domestic cats?

_____

_____

_____

_____

_____

11. What is a gestation period?

_____

_____

_____

_____

_____

12. How does the gestation period for a domestic cat compare with the gestation period for a domestic dog?

_____

_____

_____

_____

_____

13. Although humans are much larger than domestic cats, our skeletal structure contains fewer bones. How many more bones are in a cat's skeletal system?

_____

_____

_____

_____

_____

What difference do these extra bones and the joints that connect them make?

_____

_____

_____

_____

14. Read *The Little Old Woman and the Hungry Cat* by Nancy Polette. Assume that all the people in the story are 5 feet 10 inches tall and of average weight, that the horses are of the American saddle breed, that a cupcake weighs 2 1/4 ounces, and that a sewing basket weighs two pounds. How much would the hungry cat weigh after eating everything he encounters in the story?

_____

_____

_____

_____

_____

Is there any animal in existence that weighs more than this? If so, what is the animal and how much more than the hungry cat does it weigh?

_____

_____

_____

_____

_____

15. In the real world, how much did the heaviest domestic cat on record weigh? What was its name?

_____

_____

_____

_____

_____

CATS
Bibliography

Dictionary

The Guinness Book of World Records. New York: Facts on File, 1992.

Polette, Nancy. *The Little Old Woman and the Hungry Cat*. New York: Green-
willow Books, 1989.

Stolz, Mary. *Cat Walk*. New York: Harper and Row, 1983.

The World Almanac and Book of Facts. New York: World Almanac, 1992.

The World Book Encyclopedia. Chicago: World Book, Inc., 1990.

WHITE TIGERS

1. According to *National Geographic* magazine, how many white tigers did wildlife experts estimate were alive in 1989?

_____

_____

_____

_____

_____

2. According to the source used above, how many white tigers were sighted in India's jungle over a 50-year period?

_____

_____

_____

_____

_____

3. What fraction of the estimated white tiger population has been sighted over a 50-year period?

_____

_____

_____

_____

_____

What percentage is this?

_____

_____

_____

_____

4. If each country in the world wanted to adopt one white tiger, would there be enough to go around? Explain your answer.

_____

_____

_____

_____

_____

5. According to the *National Geographic* article "White Tiger in My House," what is the number of kittens a mother tiger may give birth to at a time?

_____

_____

_____

_____

How does this compare with other kinds of tigers?

_____

_____

_____

_____

6. What was the largest recorded number of young born to a wild mammal at a single birth?

_____

_____

_____

_____

_____

How does this compare with the largest recorded litter of domestic kittens?

_____

_____

_____

_____

7. Study the photographs in the article from Question 5. How much time elapsed from the time the picture was taken of white tiger kitten Rewati on pages 486-487 and the time she was relinquished to the zoo?

_____

_____

_____

_____

8. In an earlier *National Geographic* article about white tigers, the author comments about the tremendous growth of a kitten during a two-year period. How much did the kitten grow?

_____

_____

_____

_____

_____

If the kitten grew at a consistent rate, how many pounds did she gain per year?

_____

_____

_____

_____

How many pounds is this per month?

_____

_____

_____

_____

Per week?

_____

_____

_____

_____

9. If you gained the same amount of weight per year as the kitten discussed in Question 8, how much would you *weigh* five years from now?

_____

_____

_____

_____

_____

10. What is the difference between your answer to Question 9 and the weight of the largest tiger ever held in captivity?

_____

_____

_____

_____

_____

WHITE TIGERS
Bibliography

The Guinness Book of World Records. New York: Facts on File, 1992.

"Mini-explosion in White Tiger Births." *National Geographic,* Sept. 1989, Geographica section.

Reed, Elizabeth C. "White Tiger in My House." *National Geographic,* Apr. 1970, pp. 482-491.

Reed, Theodore H. "Enchantress." *National Geographic,* May 1961, pp. 628-641.

The World Almanac and Book of Facts. New York: World Almanac, 1992.

The World Book Encyclopedia. Chicago: World Book, Inc., 1990.

MONKEYS
and Other Primates

1. Describe the potto and tell where it can be found.

_____

_____

_____

_____

_____

2. It is said in African legend that pottos are so lazy that they don't take more than ten steps a day. If this legend is true and one potto step measures six inches, how many days would it take a potto to walk the width of Nigeria?

_____

_____

_____

_____

_____

3. Describe the tarsier and tell where it can be found.

_____

_____

_____

_____

_____

4. How many degrees can the tarsier turn its head?

_____

_____

_____

_____

_____

If a tarsier started looking straight ahead at you, what part of its head would you be looking at if it then turned its head this number of degrees?

_____

_____

_____

_____

5. Compare the size of a potto to the size of a tarsier by determining:

Which is taller? By how many inches?

_____

_____

_____

_____

_____

Which weighs more? By how many pounds and ounces?

_____

_____

_____

_____

6. What are two main differences between Old World and New World monkeys?

_____

_____

_____

_____

_____

7. What is the largest New World monkey? (HINT: It is known for its incredible voice.)

_____

_____

_____

_____

_____

How large is this breed?

_____

_____

_____

_____

8. When the largest New World monkey makes its call, how far away can its voice be heard?

_____

_____

_____

_____

_____

By communicating this way, how many of these monkeys would it take to send a message from the northern border of Argentina to the southern border of Mexico?

_____

_____

_____

_____

9. What kind of monkey has lived the longest in captivity? What was his name? How old was he?

_____

_____

_____

_____

How does this record compare with the average life expectancy for this breed?

_____

_____

_____

_____

10. Is it normal for this breed of monkey to be held in captivity?

_____

_____

_____

_____

11. How tall is a capuchin monkey?

_____

_____

_____

_____

12. How much smaller is a capuchin than the largest New World monkey?

_____

_____

_____

_____

13. Would you find a red howler monkey and a potto in the same jungle? Explain.

_____

_____

_____

_____

_____

14. Name at least three differences between monkeys and apes.

_____

_____

_____

_____

_____

15. From the smallest to the largest, list the four types of apes according to size.

_____

_____

_____

_____

_____

16. If you were standing next to a full grown chimpanzee, how would your sizes compare? (Discuss both weight and height.)

_____

_____

_____

_____

_____

17. Which has a longer gestation period, a chimpanzee or a gorilla?

_____

_____

_____

_____

How many days longer?

_____

_____

_____

_____

18. How often does a chimp build a new nest?

_____

_____

_____

_____

How many nests would a chimp in the wild build in an average lifetime?

_____

_____

_____

_____

19. Animals in captivity often behave differently from those in their natural surroundings. Assume, however, that a chimp in captivity and one in the wild *would* behave in the same way and that both had the same nesting materials available to them. Would the number of nests the captive chimp built in a lifetime be the same as that of the chimp in its natural habitat? Explain.

_____

_____

_____

_____

_____

20. What was the greatest authenticated age to which any primate has ever lived? In what country was this record set?

_____

_____

_____

_____

_____

On what date will the oldest living human tie this record?

_____

_____

_____

_____

21. Why do you think biological laboratories use chimpanzees to test drugs and surgical techniques intended for humans?

_____

_____

_____

_____

_____

22. How do you feel about the use of animals in this type of testing? Explain your answer.

_____

_____

_____

_____

_____

MONKEYS and Other Primates
Bibliography

Atlas

Dictionary

Gelman, Rita Golden. *Monkeys and Apes of the World*. New York: Franklin Watts, 1990.

The Guinness Book of World Records. New York: Facts on File, 1992.

Lemmon, Tess. *Monkeys*. New York: Bookwright Press, 1992.

The Marshall Cavandish International Wildlife Encyclopedia. Freeport, Long Island: Marshall Cavandish Corp., 1989.

Petty, Kate. *Chimpanzees*. New York: Gloucester Press, 1990.

Stone, Lynn M. *Chimpanzees*. Vero Beach, FL: Rourke Corp., Inc., 1990.

Wexo, John Bonnett. *The Apes*. Mankato, MN: Creative Education, 1990.

The World Book Encyclopedia. Chicago: World Book, Inc., 1990.

* * *

We also found the following out-of-print resources useful. We include these resources for those who may have them in their collections.

Allen, Martha Dickson. *Meet the Monkeys*. Englewood Cliffs, NJ: Prentice-Hall, Inc., 1979.

Monkeys and Apes. New York: Time-Life Films, Inc., 1976.

Whitlock, Ralph. *Chimpanzees*. Milwaukee: Raintree Childrens Books, 1977.

PENGUINS

1. What is the average number of eggs most kinds of penguins lay at a time?

_____

_____

_____

_____

_____

2. How many eggs does the female Emperor penguin lay?

_____

_____

_____

_____

_____

3. What is unusual about the care of the Emperor penguin's egg?

_____

_____

_____

_____

_____

4. How many hours does it take for an Emperor penguin's egg to hatch?

_____

_____

_____

_____

How many minutes is this?

_____

_____

_____

5. About how many pounds does the adult male Emperor penguin weigh when the egg hatches?

_____

_____

_____

_____

6. If you took a magnifying glass and examined a penguin's coat, about how many feathers might you find growing in an area the size of a postage stamp (approximately one square inch)?

_____

_____

_____

_____

7. If you were to examine an area of a penguin's coat equal to an array of postage stamps five stamps high and seven stamps wide, how many feathers would you find?

_____

_____

_____

_____

8. Using your answer from Question 7, how many feathers do you estimate cover an adult Emperor penguin?

_____

_____

_____

_____

How did you determine this number?

_____

_____

_____

How does your estimate compare with the highest feather count recorded for any species?

_____

_____

_____

_____

9. How often do penguins molt? What does "molt" mean?

_____

_____

_____

_____

10. Why do penguins stay on land during molting?

_____

_____

_____

_____

11. According to a *3-2-1 Contact* article about a "penguin paradise," how long have the penguins at Sea World's Penguin Encounter been there?

_____

_____

_____

_____

12. How much snow do the keepers at Sea World's Penguin En-counter make each day?

_____

_____

_____

_____

How much snow is made each hour?

_____

_____

_____

_____

How much is made each minute?

_____

_____

_____

_____

Each second?

_____

_____

_____

_____

13. How much snow is made at the Encounter each year?

_____

_____

_____

_____

14. How much snow have the keepers at the Encounter made since their project began?

_____

_____

_____

_____

15. How much snow has been made since Ann Bowles has been watching the colony at the Encounter?

_____

_____

_____

_____

16. Approximately how many years ago did explorers first see penguins, according to the article mentioned in Question 11?

_____

_____

_____

_____

17. If you saw a penguin for the first time, what would you think it was, a bird or a fish? Explain.

_____

_____

_____

_____

_____

18. How long did Ann Bowles work at the Encounter before the penguin King Tut was born?

_____

_____

_____

_____

_____

19. How deep do Emperor penguins usually dive?

_____

_____

_____

_____

_____

20. How does this compare with the deepest recorded dive for a group of Emperor penguins?

_____

_____

_____

_____

_____

21. The *3-2-1 Contact* article from Question 11 mentioned the way penguins work together. Describe this.

_____

_____

_____

_____

_____

    Even animals that are different can become partners to accomplish something by working together. Find two examples of this.

_____

_____

_____

_____

PENGUINS
Bibliography

Arnold, Caroline. *Penguin.* New York: Morrow Junior Books, 1988.

Barrett, Norman. *Penguins.* New York: Franklin Watts, 1991.

Dictionary

The Guinness Book of World Records. New York: Facts on File, 1992.

The Marshall Cavandish International Wildlife Encyclopedia. Freeport, Long Island: Marshall Cavandish Corp., 1989.

"Penguin Pin-Up." *3-2-1 Contact,* Jan./Feb. 1990, pp. 24-35.

Rosen, Sybil and Eric Weiner. "Penguin Paradise: An Ice Place to Visit!" *3-2-1 Contact,* Jan./Feb. 1990, pp. 20-23.

Strange, Ian J. *Penguin World.* New York: Dodd, Mead and Co., 1981.

Wexo, John Bonnett. *Penguins.* Mankato, MN: Creative Education, Inc., 1990.

The World Book Encyclopedia. Chicago: World Book, Inc., 1990.

* * *

We also found the following out-of-print resources useful. We include these resources for those who may have them in their collections.

Crow, Sandra Lee. *Penguins and Polar Bears: Animals of Ice and Snow.* Washington, DC: National Geographic Society, 1985.

Tenaza, Richard. *Penguins.* New York: Franklin Watts, 1980.

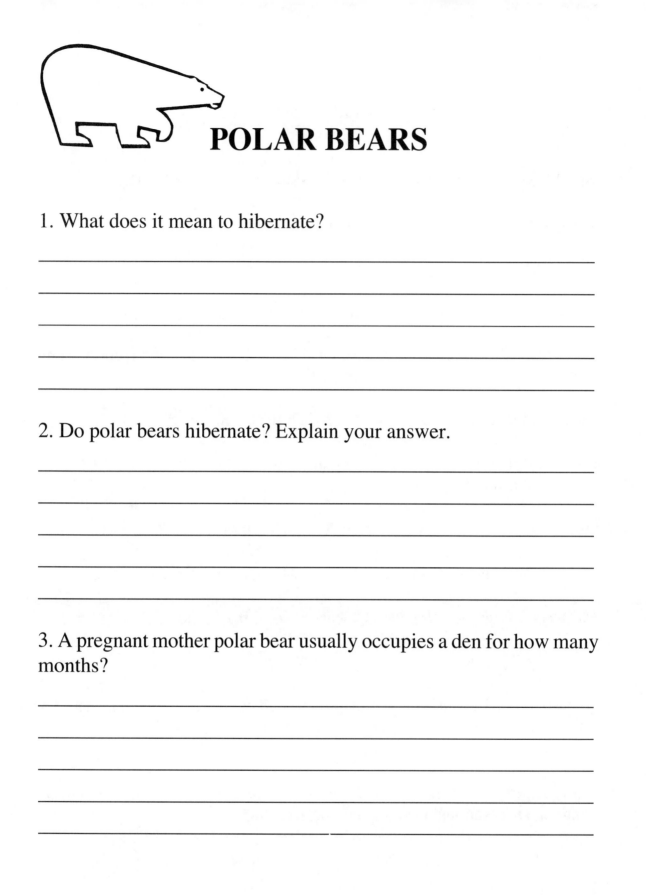

POLAR BEARS

1. What does it mean to hibernate?

_____

_____

_____

_____

_____

2. Do polar bears hibernate? Explain your answer.

_____

_____

_____

_____

_____

3. A pregnant mother polar bear usually occupies a den for how many months?

_____

_____

_____

_____

_____

How many days is this?

_____

_____

_____

_____

4. Approximately how many months does a polar bear's gestation period last?

_____

_____

_____

_____

_____

How many days is this?

_____

_____

_____

_____

5. On average, how many cubs will a polar bear mother give birth to as the result of a single pregnancy?

_____

_____

_____

_____

_____

6. Describe polar bear cubs at birth.

_____

_____

_____

_____

7. A polar bear begins to hear at 26 days. How many more days will it take before its hearing becomes perfect?

_____

_____

_____

_____

_____

8. How many months old is a polar bear cub before it starts to walk?

_____

_____

_____

_____

How does this compare to a human baby?

_____

_____

_____

_____

9. How many days old is a polar bear cub when it first begins to see?

_____

_____

_____

_____

_____

How many weeks is this?

_____

_____

_____

_____

How many months?

_____

_____

_____

_____

10. How many months old are the cubs before they leave the den for the first time?

_____

_____

_____

_____

11. Approximately how much do polar bears weigh at birth?

_____

_____

_____

_____

_____

When they emerge from the den for the first time, how much weight have the cubs *gained?*

_____

_____

_____

_____

12. How many months do the cubs stay with their mother?

_____

_____

_____

_____

_____

How many weeks is this?

_____

_____

_____

_____

How many days?

_____

_____

_____

_____

13. Make a timetable of the development of a polar bear from the time of its birth to the time it leaves its mother.

_____

_____

_____

_____

_____

14. Compare the size of an adult male polar bear to that of adult males of at least two other kinds of bears.

_____

_____

_____

_____

_____

15. What is the difference in height between an adult male polar bear and an adult female polar bear?

_____

_____

_____

_____

_____

Name another species that is approximately the same height as a female polar bear.

_____

_____

_____

_____

16. From how many feet away can a polar bear smell food?

_____

_____

_____

_____

_____

How many inches is this?

_____

_____

_____

_____

17. How many Emperor penguins would it take to make one full meal for a polar bear? Is it likely that a polar bear would eat a penguin in the wild? Explain.

_____

_____

_____

_____

18. How many feet from land have polar bears been seen swimming?

_____

_____

_____

_____

_____

19. A polar bear usually does not travel more than about 125 miles from its population center. If a polar bear can travel this distance in any direction from this center, what is the maximum number of square miles he could cover?

_____

_____

_____

_____

_____

How many square feet is this?

_____

_____

_____

_____

20. In the early 1960s, approximately how many polar bears did scientists estimate remained in the world?

_____

_____

_____

_____

21. Approximately how many polar bears were estimated to exist by the end of the 1980s?

_____

_____

_____

_____

22. How has the polar bear population changed since the 1960s? Why do you think this change has occurred?

_____

_____

_____

_____

23. On average, how long do polar bears in the wild live?

_____

_____

_____

_____

24. On average, how long do captive polar bears live?

_____

_____

_____

_____

How do you explain this difference?

_____

_____

_____

_____

POLAR BEARS
Bibliography

Bright, Michael. *Polar Bear*. New York: Gloucester Press, 1989.

Dictionary

The Marshall Cavandish International Wildlife Encyclopedia. Freeport, Long Island: Marshall Cavandish Corp., 1989.

The World Book Encyclopedia. Chicago: World Book, Inc., 1990.

* * *

We also found the following out-of-print resource useful. We include this resource for those who may have it in their collections.

Crow, Sandra Lee. *Penguins and Polar Bears: Animals of Ice and Snow*. Washington, DC: National Geographic Society, 1985.

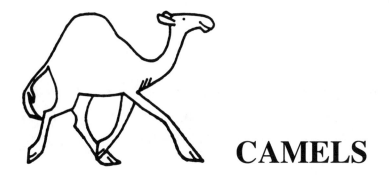 **CAMELS**

1. According to Rudyard Kipling's *Just So Stories*, why was the camel given a hump?

_____

_____

_____

_____

_____

2. In the story, what purpose did the hump serve?

_____

_____

_____

_____

_____

3. Does the camel's hump really serve this purpose? Explain.

_____

_____

_____

_____

4. In a Christmas story about a camel written by Nancy Parker, a boy receives a pet camel from Cairo, Egypt. If the boy in the story lives in New York City, how far does the camel have to be transported to get to the boy's home?

_____

_____

_____

_____

_____

5. How long can a camel go without water?

_____

_____

_____

_____

How many weeks is this?

_____

_____

_____

_____

How many hours is this?

_____

_____

_____

_____

6. How much water could a dromedary drink in ten minutes if it had been without water for a long time?

_____

_____

_____

_____

_____

       How much water would that be per minute?

_____

_____

_____

_____

7. In two other sources, discover how much water a dehydrated camel can drink.

_____

_____

_____

_____

       How does the information in these sources compare?

_____

_____

_____

_____

If the information is different in the two sources, why do you think this is so?

_____

_____

_____

_____

8. Describe how a dehydrated camel's appearance changes after drinking a large quantity of water.

_____

_____

_____

_____

_____

9. During the journey mentioned in a 1978 *National Geographic* article about a trip across Australia, camels were used to carry loads of 500 pounds each. Is this the same weight that average working camels carry when traveling a long distance? Explain.

_____

_____

_____

_____

_____

10. What is the average number of days required to make a 1,700 mile trip across Australia's wilderness riding a camel?

_____

_____

_____

_____

How many days would it take to cover the same ground riding a fast dromedary?

_____

_____

_____

_____

11. How many years ago did people start using camels in Australia?

_____

_____

_____

_____

12. In the 1920s, camels were used less frequently in the outback. Why?

_____

_____

_____

_____

13. Compare the total number of toes a camel has with the total number a horse has.

_____

_____

_____

_____

14. Name at least one other animal that has the same number of toes as a camel.

_____

_____

_____

_____

_____

15. If a 1,500-pound camel loses 550 pounds, is it in danger of distress? Explain.

_____

_____

_____

_____

_____

16. How much weight can a 1,000-pound camel lose without suffering any ill effects?

_____

_____

_____

_____

_____

17. Give the fraction that represents the weight of a camel's hump compared to its total body weight.

_____

_____

_____

_____

_____

18. From your research about camels, how would you describe their behavior?

_____

_____

_____

_____

_____

Are your feelings about camel behavior the same as those Robyn Davidson expressed in the article mentioned in Question 9? Explain.

_____

_____

_____

_____

CAMELS
Bibliography

Atlas

Davidson, Robyn. "Alone Across the Outback." *National Geographic,* May 1978, pp. 581-611.

Dictionary

Kipling, Rudyard. *Just So Stories.* (Any edition which includes "How the Camel Got Its Hump.")

Machotka, Hana. *What Neat Feet!* New York: Morrow, 1991.

The Marshall Cavandish International Wildlife Encyclopedia. Freeport, Long Island: Marshall Cavandish Corp., 1989. (Or other edition)

Parnall, Peter. *Feet!* New York: Macmillan, 1988.

Wexo, John Bonnett. *Camels.* Mankato, MN: Creative Education, 1989.

The World Book Encyclopedia. Chicago: World Book, Inc., 1990.

* * *

We also found the following out-of-print resources useful. We include these resources for those who may have them in their collections.

Cloudsley-Thompson, John. *Camels.* Milwaukee: Raintree Childrens Books, 1980.

Parker, Nancy Winslow. *The Christmas Camel.* New York: Dodd, Mead and Co., 1983.

GIRAFFES

1. How long have the giraffe's ancestors been on earth?

_____

_____

_____

_____

_____

2. According to *The Giraffe That Walked to Paris,* how many years ago did the first giraffe arrive in France?

_____

_____

_____

_____

_____

3. If the king's giraffe took the most direct route from Marseilles to Paris, approximately how many miles did it walk each day?

_____

_____

_____

_____

_____

To what cities other than Paris could the giraffe have gone travelling the same distance from Marseilles?

_____

_____

_____

_____

4. During the giraffe's journey across the sea from Egypt to Marseilles, how many gallons of milk were needed to feed it for two weeks if each bucket held 2.6 gallons?

_____

_____

_____

_____

_____

About how many gallons of milk did each cow have to supply?

_____

_____

_____

_____

5. How does the life span of the first giraffe to arrive in France compare with the estimated life span of giraffes?

_____

_____

_____

_____

_____

6. If the first giraffe to arrive in the United States was still alive today, how many average giraffe lifetimes would it already have lived?

_____

_____

_____

_____

_____

7. Should a giraffe in captivity or a giraffe in the wild have a longer life span? Why?

_____

_____

_____

_____

_____

8. How many months long is the giraffe's gestation period?

_____

_____

_____

_____

_____

How many days is this?

_____

_____

_____

_____

9. How many human babies could be born in the same time that it takes one giraffe to be born, from the time of conception to the time of birth?

_____

_____

_____

_____

_____

10. If 48 wild giraffe calves were born in Africa on the same day, how many would be likely to die within one year?

_____

_____

_____

_____

_____

11. Give the fraction (in lowest terms) that compares a baby giraffe's height to the height of a full grown giraffe bull.

_____

_____

_____

_____

_____

12. To what height will a baby giraffe grow in its first year?

_____

_____

_____

_____

_____

13. How many years does it take for a giraffe to be fully grown?

_____

_____

_____

_____

_____

14. On average, how many feet (in height) does a giraffe grow per year between the time it is one year old and the time it is fully grown?

_____

_____

_____

_____

_____

15. How many feet long is a giraffe's tongue?

_____

_____

_____

_____

How many inches is this?

_____

_____

_____

_____

16. How many feet long is a giraffe's tail?

_____

_____

_____

_____

_____

How many inches is this?

_____

_____

_____

_____

17. Give the fractional weight (in lowest terms) of a giraffe bull's skull compared to his total body weight.

_____

_____

_____

_____

_____

18. Give the fractional weight (in lowest terms) of the cow's skull compared to her total body weight.

_____

_____

_____

_____

_____

19. How many fourth graders would it take to equal the weight of a full grown giraffe bull? (Use the average weight in your group.)

_____

_____

_____

_____

_____

20. Name two mammals that are heavier than a giraffe.

_____

_____

_____

_____

_____

21. How many fourth graders would it take to equal the height of a full grown giraffe bull? (Use the average height in your group.)

_____

_____

_____

_____

_____

22. Name an animal other than a giraffe that is in the *giraffidae* family.

_____

_____

_____

_____

_____

23. What part or parts of the animal you named in Question 22 resemble(s) a giraffe?

_____

_____

_____

_____

_____

24. Early man thought that the giraffe was made by putting together body parts of many animals. What animals, other than the one you discussed in Question 22, have features similar to those of the giraffe?

_____

_____

_____

_____

_____

25. One of the giraffe's favorite foods comes from the acacia tree. If each acacia cluster weighs 1/8 of a pound, how many clusters must a giraffe normally eat in a 24-hour period to fulfill its daily food requirements?

_____

_____

_____

_____

26. The giraffe shares a special partnership with another animal. Name the animal and explain how this partnership is helpful to both.

_____

_____

_____

_____

_____

27. Some people say the giraffe is a work of art that has taken nature millions of years to refine so that it can survive. What makes the giraffe a work of art?

_____

_____

_____

_____

28. Over the years, how has the giraffe adapted for survival?

_____

_____

_____

_____

_____

GIRAFFES
Bibliography

Atlas

Dictionary

The Marshall Cavandish International Wildlife Encyclopedia. Freeport, Long
    Island: Marshall Cavandish Corp., 1989.

Milton, Nancy. *The Giraffe That Walked to Paris*. New York: Crown Publish-
    ers, Inc., 1992.

Sattler, Helen Roney. *Giraffes, the Sentinels of the Savannas*. New York:
    Lothrop, Lee and Shepard Books, 1989.

Stone, Lynn M. *Giraffes*. Vero Beach, FL: Rourke Corp., Inc., 1990.

The World Book Encyclopedia. Chicago: World Book, Inc., 1990.

* * *

We also found the following out-of-print resource useful. We include this re-
    source for those who may have it in their collections.

Schlein, Miriam. *Giraffe: The Silent Giant*. New York: Four Winds Press,
    1976.

GRIZZLY BEARS

1. Find a children's magazine article entitled "The Tale of Hugh Glass and the Grizzly." How many years ago did Glass encounter Old Ephraim?

_____

_____

_____

_____

_____

2. If each step that Glass took (after he shot Old Ephraim once) measured three feet, how many feet had Glass gone before the bear caught up with him?

_____

_____

_____

_____

_____

3. How much money did the expedition leader offer as a bonus to volunteers who agreed to stay behind with Glass?

_____

_____

_____

_____

_____

4. If the amount of money offered to volunteers was 1/40 the price of a new house, how much would a new house cost?

_____

_____

_____

_____

_____

5. If the bonus money was nearly three months' pay, about how much was one month's pay?

_____

_____

_____

_____

_____

6. Based on the calculation above, what was a year's pay?

_____

_____

_____

_____

7. How many hours did Glass stay at the spring before moving on?

_____

_____

_____

_____

_____

8. If Glass moved 48 feet per hour, how many hours would it have taken him to travel one mile?

_____

_____

_____

_____

_____

9. If Glass traveled for 12 hours each day, what was the average distance he needed to cover each hour to complete one mile by the end of the day?

_____

_____

_____

_____

_____

10. How many days did it take Glass to travel 100 miles?

_____

_____

_____

_____

11. What was the average distance Glass traveled per day?

_____

_____

_____

_____

12. According to the *National Geographic* article, " 'Grizz'—Of Men and the Great Bear," are grizzly attacks on humans a common occurrence? Explain your answer.

_____

_____

_____

_____

13. According to the article from Question 12, how many years have grizzly bears been listed as endangered?

_____

_____

_____

_____

14. From the same article, how many grizzlies were killed per year between the years 1968 and 1973 as a result of interaction with people?

_____

_____

_____

_____

_____

15. In 1986, how many grizzlies lived in 5.7 million acres in Montana?

_____

_____

_____

_____

How many grizzlies is this per million acres?

_____

_____

_____

_____

16. If the number of grizzlies mentioned in Question 15 represented 30% of the grizzly population, how many grizzlies were estimated to be alive in the lower 48 states during 1986?

_____

_____

_____

_____

_____

17. In what year did Yellowstone National Park close its garbage dumps?

_____

_____

_____

_____

_____

18. Between the time that Yellowstone National Park closed its dumps and 1986, what was the reduction in the number of grizzlies per year?

_____

_____

_____

_____

19. If Yellowstone kept losing grizzlies at the same rate as in Question 18, how many would be in the park today?

_____

_____

_____

_____

_____

20. In addition to the decreasing number of adult grizzlies, the number of cubs per litter also has declined. By how much have the litters declined?

_____

_____

_____

_____

_____

21. According to what you have read about grizzly interaction with people in the Yellowstone area, why do you think it would be wise to adopt a "do not feed the animals" policy?

_____

_____

_____

_____

GRIZZLY BEARS
Bibliography

Chadwick, Douglas H. " 'Grizz'—Of Men and the Great Bear." *National Geographic,* Feb. 1986, pp. 182-213.

Dictionary

Hardee, Jim. "The Tale of Hugh Glass and the Grizzly." *Boys' Life,* Nov. 1989, p. 16.

ELEPHANTS

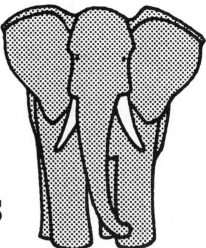

1. What two species of elephants are in existence today?

_____

_____

_____

_____

Name at least five ways they are different from each other.

_____

_____

_____

_____

2. What was the name of the most famous circus elephant?

_____

_____

_____

_____

3. Before this elephant was purchased for the circus, how much time did it spend in the London Zoo?

_____

_____

_____

_____

_____

How many years ago was it purchased by P.T. Barnum?

_____

_____

_____

_____

4. Who was P.T. Barnum?

_____

_____

_____

_____

_____

What was his famous quote?

_____

_____

_____

_____

What do you think he meant?

_____

_____

_____

_____

_____

5. Why is it surprising that this circus elephant was of the African species?

_____

_____

_____

_____

_____

6. Compare this circus elephant's height to the standing height of the largest elephant ever recorded.

_____

_____

_____

_____

_____

Compare their weights in pounds.

_____

_____

_____

_____

7. What is a short ton?

_____

_____

_____

_____

_____

8. The height of an elephant is about equal to its length. Equal dimensions can also form a perfect square. Extend your arms so that they are horizontal to the floor. Measure the length of your reach, then compare this measurement to your height. Do this for all members in your group to find if anyone's measurements would make a perfect square.

_____

_____

_____

_____

_____

9. How much food does an elephant eat each day? Find answers to this question from three different sources.

_____

_____

_____

_____

_____

How does the information from these sources compare?

_____

_____

_____

_____

Why do you think this information varies?

_____

_____

_____

_____

10. Determine the average of your answers from Question 9. Then determine from this number how many pounds of food it would take to feed an elephant for a week?

_____

_____

_____

_____

_____

For a month?

_____

_____

_____

_____

A year?

_____

_____

_____

_____

During an average elephant lifetime?

_____

_____

_____

_____

11. List at least three factors that determine an elephant's life span.

_____

_____

_____

_____

12. An elephant grows six sets of molars in a lifetime. How many teeth does this total?

_____

_____

_____

_____

13. How many elephant molars would it take to equal the weight of each of your group members?

_____

_____

_____

_____

14. At what age does the elephant's last set of molars appear?

_____

_____

_____

_____

Assuming that the other five sets of molars grow in at regular intervals, at what ages would an elephant get each new set of molars?

_____

_____

_____

15. What fractional amount of the adult male African elephant's (bull's) weight is contained in his tusks?

_____

_____

_____

_____

16. Just as only the top part of a human's teeth can be seen, only part of an elephant's tusks are exposed. About how many inches of an adult African bull's tusk is hidden?

_____

_____

_____

_____

_____

17. If all of the members of your group were squeezed into a hollow log that weighed 50 pounds, could an elephant lift the log with all of you in it?

_____

_____

_____

_____

_____

18. How many times would an elephant have to fill its trunk with water to empty the largest land-locked, heated swimming pool?

_____

_____

_____

_____

19. For what length of time do mother elephants look after their young?

_____

_____

_____

_____

_____

What is the only mammal that cares for its young longer than the elephant?

_____

_____

_____

_____

20. Like some other animal species, elephants travel in herds. What family member is dominant in the herd?

_____

_____

_____

_____

_____

Name one other species in which this family member also dominates.

_____

_____

_____

_____

21. In a 1989 *National Geographic* article about elephant communication, researchers electronically recorded the sounds made by a group of elephants during a one-month period, then printed out their results. How many elephant calls were recorded on their printout?

_____

_____

_____

_____

What number of the recorded calls had the scientists actually heard?

_____

_____

_____

_____

22. According to the article above, how many sounds were recorded over a two-and-a-half-month period?

_____

_____

_____

_____

_____

Assume that the researchers actually heard the same percentage of the calls they had recorded over two and a half months as they had heard of the calls recorded over one month. Approximately how many of the calls recorded over the longer period did the scientists *not* hear?

_____

_____

_____

_____

23. Find 1980 and 1991 *National Geographic* articles about elephants. Each of these two articles contains a map showing estimated elephant distribution throughout Africa. Study these maps and choose ten African countries. Compare the number of elephants said to exist in these countries during each study. In making these comparisons, organize your findings in the form of a chart.

_____

_____

_____

_____

_____

_____

_____

_____

_____

_____

24. Study your chart from the previous page. How have the elephant populations in each country changed over the years?

_____

_____

_____

_____

_____

What do these changes suggest to you?

_____

_____

_____

_____

25. What percentage of the world's existing elephant population inhabits Asia?

_____

_____

_____

_____

_____

26. On the average, how many African elephants were lost per year between 1979 and 1989?

_____

_____

_____

_____

_____

27. At the turn of this century perhaps 200,000 elephants inhabited Asia. On the average, how many elephants were lost per year between that time and 1989?

_____

_____

_____

_____

_____

28. Using a *National Geographic* update published in 1988 and the 1991 article from Question 23, find the elephant population in Kenya for four different years. Arrange this information in a table listing the most recent data first.

_____

_____

_____

_____

_____

29. Find the average reduction in numbers of elephants per year between each two consecutive listings on your timetable from above.

_____

_____

_____

_____

_____

How has the rate changed over the years?

_____

_____

_____

_____

30. What is culling?

_____

_____

_____

_____

How is it used in relation to elephant populations?

_____

_____

_____

_____

How do you feel about this?

_____

_____

_____

_____

31. According to the update from Question 28, what number of elephants are killed legally each year?

_____

_____

_____

_____

_____

How many are killed illegally?

_____

_____

_____

_____

32. Considering everything you have read about this topic, what is the greatest threat to elephant survival? Explain.

_____

_____

_____

_____

_____

ELEPHANTS
Bibliography

Bartlett, John. *Bartlett's Familiar Quotations*. Boston: Little, Brown and Co., 1982.

Blumberg, Rhoda. *Jumbo*. New York: Bradbury Press, 1992.

Bright, Michael. *Elephants*. New York: Gloucester Press, 1990.

Chadwick, Douglas H. "Elephants—Out of Time, Out of Space." *National Geographic,* May 1991, pp. 2-49.

Dictionary

Douglas-Hamilton, Oria. "Africa's Elephants: Can They Survive?" *National Geographic,* Nov. 1980, pp. 568-603.

"Elephant Update." *National Geographic,* Oct. 1988, Geographica section.

The Guinness Book of World Records. New York: Facts on File, 1992.

The Marshall Cavandish International Wildlife Encyclopedia. Freeport, Long Island: Marshall Cavandish Corp., 1989.

Payne, Katharine. *Elephants Calling*. New York: Crown Publishers, Inc., 1992.

Payne, Katharine. "Elephant Talk." *National Geographic,* Aug. 1989, pp. 264-277.

Petty, Kate. *Elephants*. New York: Gloucester Press, 1990.

Redmond, Ian. *Elephants*. New York: Bookwright Press, 1990.

Wexo, John Bonnett. *Elephants*. Mankato, MN: Creative Education, 1989.

The World Book Encyclopedia. Chicago: World Book, Inc., 1990.

INDEXES

Children's Magazine Guide. New York: R.R. Bowker.

National Geographic Index. Washington, DC: National Geographic Society.

OTHER ENCYCLOPEDIAS
Used by Students in Our Library

Children's Britannica. Chicago: Encyclopaedia Britannica, Inc.

The Merit Student Encyclopedia. New York: MacMillan Educational Co.

The New Book of Knowledge. Danbury, CT: Grolier, Inc.

The New Grolier Student Encyclopedia. Danbury, CT: Grolier Educational Corp.

Mammals: A Multimedia Encyclopedia (CD-ROM). National Geographic Society. Washington, DC, 1990.

ZOOLUTIONS SUPPLIES

Almanac

Atlas

Card Catalog or On-Line Catalog

Cat Walk **by Mary Stolz**

Children's Magazine Guide

The Church Mouse **by Graham Oakley**

Dictionary

General Encyclopedia

The Guinness Book of World Records

Monkeys and Apes of the World **by Rita Golden Gelman**

National Geographic Index

Penguin **by Caroline Arnold**

Wildlife Encyclopedia

(This Zoolutions Supplies list should be distributed with all animal topics.)

GROUP CHECKLIST
FOR COOPERATIVE BEHAVIORS

Did everyone . . .

____ share materials?

____ contribute ideas?

____ ask questions when things were unclear?

____ listen attentively when others were talking?

____ acknowledge all suggestions?

____ encourage all members of the group to participate?

____ check to see that all members understood each question and its solution?

____ help give the group direction and focus, keeping the discussion to our topic?

____ speak in a soft voice?

____ help make sure each problem was solved as a group?

Appendix C

STUDENT WRITING SAMPLES

NOTE: Spelling corrections have been made and student names have been changed.

Student #1   Topic: Great Lakes Fish

Our question we answered today was "How much money did the U.S. spend each year in purifying the Great Lakes since Truchan was born?"

We divided the amount of money the U.S. used in total by the age of Truchan. That would mean dividing $4,000,000,000 by 47. We came up with $85,106,382 per year.

Conclusion: That means that the U.S. spent a total of $85,106,382 per year in purifying the Great Lakes water since Truchan was born. Now I know how the budget deficit got so big!

We finished this problem after you helped us. We are doing very good on Great Lakes Fish. Too bad Kyle and Gary's group got Elephants.

Student #2   Topic: Monkeys

In Zoolutions on Monday, we were asked how many howler monkeys would it take to call from the southern border of Mexico to the northern border of Argentina. We looked through several atlases with no luck. My two companions were trying to figure it out the wrong way. They (or at least one of them) thought that we needed to figure out how big Mexico was and how big Argentina was, then add them together and divide them by the number of miles a howler can call, which we found out to be two.

I disagreed because there are places in between the two countries. I finally convinced them what to do: Find the number of miles between Mexico and Argentina and divide by the number of miles a howler can call.

In an atlas, we found that there are 1,200 miles between Mexico and Argentina and we divided it by two.

In conclusion, it would take around 600 howlers to call from the bottom of Mexico to the top of Argentina.

I think our group all contributed ideas and we understood the mistakes we made.

118

Student #3   Topic: Domestic Cats

Today my group finished a part of our question. We found that an American Saddle horse weighs 1,050 pounds so we multiplied that by four because that's how many horses there were in <u>The Little Old Woman and the Hungry Cat</u> and got the answer, 4,200.

Then we had the question, if each cupcake weighs 2 1/4 ounces, how much do 16 cupcakes weigh? We found that an ounce is equal to 1/16 of a pound. So 16/16 equals 1 or a whole. There were 16 cupcakes and we drew 16 cupcakes and each one equals 2 1/4 ounces and we divided them into four equal parts. We then multiplied 2 1/4 X 4 and did that 4 times. We came up with the answer that 16 cupcakes weigh 36 ounces. We divided that by 16 ounces and found that 16 cupcakes weigh 2 1/4 lbs.

Student #4 Topic: Elephants

Today in Zoolutions my group got all "yes" on the group checklist. Even in a double period, we didn't have our usual problems like yelling or talking about unrelated topics. We worked excellently together today.

One of our questions today was, "How many elephant molars equal the weight of each of our group members?" Our first step in solving this was going down to the equipment room to weigh ourselves. We found that Dean weighs 118 pounds, Roger weighs 66 pounds, and I weigh 56 pounds. When we got back to the library, I looked in the <u>World Book Encyclopedia</u>, our faithful resource, and found that JUST ONE elephant molar weighs 8 1/2 POUNDS! Then we divided 56 (my weight) by 8 1/2 pounds and got about 6.5. I started thinking. If Roger's weight was 10 pounds more than mine, about one more molar would equal Roger's weight. About 7.75 elephant molars equal Roger's weight. My weight multiplied by two is 112. Six more pounds would be Dean's weight, so 6.5 (the number of elephant molars in my weight) times two plus about one gives the answer for Dean's weight, so about 13.25 elephant molars equal Dean's weight.

Our conclusion is that 6.5 elephant molars weigh as much as I do, 7.75 elephant molars weigh as much as Roger does, and 13.25 elephant molars weigh as much as Dean does.

Student #5 Topic: Elephants

Today in Zoolutions, my group worked on the question, "What fractional amount of an elephant's tusk is hidden by skin?" We didn't find the answer, but our strategy was to find how long an elephant's tusk is, and either how much is hidden by skin or how much sticks out.

We looked in several encyclopedias, and several non-fiction books. I learned how brutal elephant poachers are. Clark showed me a picture of a room literally stuffed with elephant tusks. It seemed that half of the elephant population's tusks were in there. In another book it shows a table covered with jewelry made from the ivory of elephant tusks. I think that poachers should make fake ivory out of plastic.

I also learned that the record for the longest tusk ever is 11.5 feet long!

Student #6   Topics: Elephants/Penguins

This year in Zoolutions, I learned a lot about the different animals I studied. Before Zoolutions, I never knew about Jumbo the elephant. In Zoolutions I not only learned who he was, I learned that he was at one time the biggest captive animal in the world. He was 11 feet tall! It is interesting that as a child, Jumbo was scrawny and wasn't very big. I also learned that African elephant's ears are shaped roughly like a map of Africa, while the Indian (Asiatic) elephant's ears are shaped roughly like a map of India. They seem like they are to scale. The African elephant's ears are about as much bigger than Africa is compared to India.

One of my favorite things I learned was that elephants have an inefficient digestive system, so they have to eat twice the amount of food their bodies need.

In Penguins, my favorite question was the one that talked about how much snow is made in a second, minute, hour, day, week, month, year and since the project began at Sea World's Penguin Encounter. If it snowed that much, school would be cancelled for a *looooooooooooooooooooooooooooong* time.

Student #7   Topic: Elephants

Today was our last day of Zoolutions. Kyle, Gary and I were trying to answer our questions the best we could. The problems that we did were all continuations from Question #10. It asked how many pounds of food will an elephant eat in a day. We had averaged the three different answers that we got from Question #9. But now we had to find the average of the averages. So we averaged our numbers. Then we had to multiply it by 7 because it asked how many pounds in a week. So we multiplied 591 and 7.

Then the next question was a continuation of the last. It asked how many in a month. We counted 30 days for a month. So we multiplied 30 and 591. Then it asked how many pounds in a year. So we multiplied 365 by 591.

Then was the big challenge. How many in an average lifetime? We looked up the elephant's average lifetime in the encyclopedia. Then we multiplied that by 591. It took a very long time just to do that one problem because the numbers we had to multiply were in the hundred thousands. (This was the only problem that I remembered the answer to.) The answer was 14,021,475 pounds of food. Fourteen million, twenty-one thousand, four hundred and seventy-five pounds of food in an elephant's lifetime! ! !

Today our group has worked harder than ever. We had absolutely no problems. The only thing that we were disappointed about was that this was our last day of Zoolutions.

Student #8   Zoolutions Summary

Today in Zoolutions was our last Zoolutions period. Altogether my group did Penguins, Camels, Great Lakes Fish, and started White Tigers.

I learned a lot in Zoolutions. I learned long division, how to use references, and a lot about animals. I learned that a camel has only two toes, I learned that the King and Emperor penguins incubate their eggs, that there is a lot of pollution in the Great Lakes, that white tigers grow to weigh about 190 pounds in two years, and a lot more.

I think that my group worked together well and that we will be able to adopt a rare animal when we combine timbala with Bert's group.

Right now I think that it is strange that I remember the first time in Zoolutions period when everybody in my group had no idea what they were doing and that now we know how to do everything really well. I learned about how to use a lot of different math and the other people in my group taught me some neat ways of doing things. Ways that I probably would never have thought of myself.

I am a little sad that we have to stop Zoolutions now because it was always one of my favorite subjects. But the good thing is that all the fun work paid off because now we get to adopt our animals.

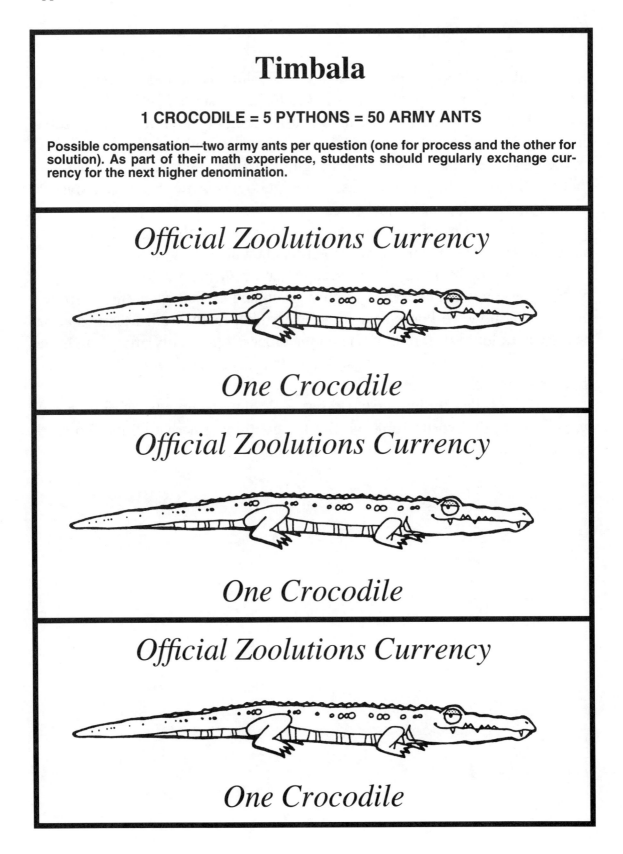

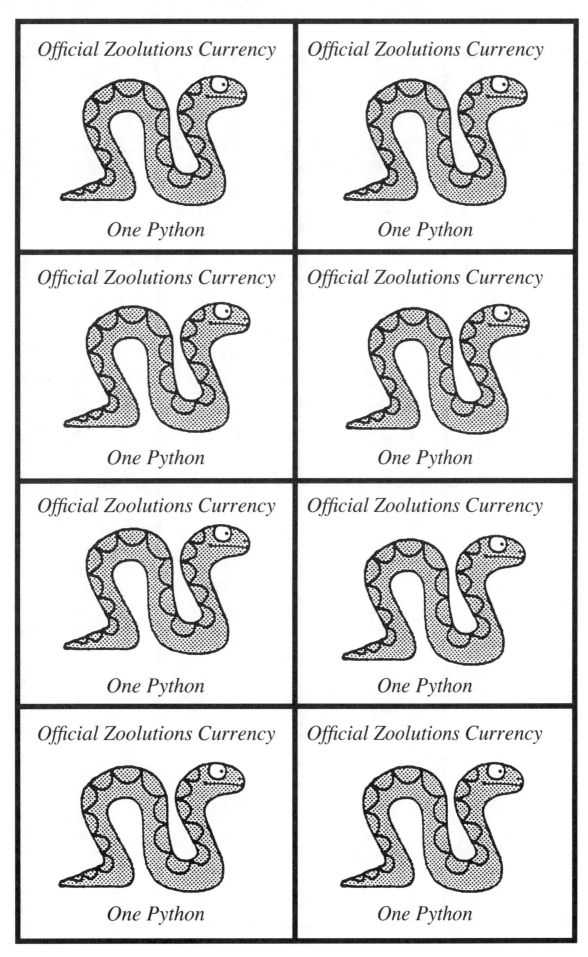

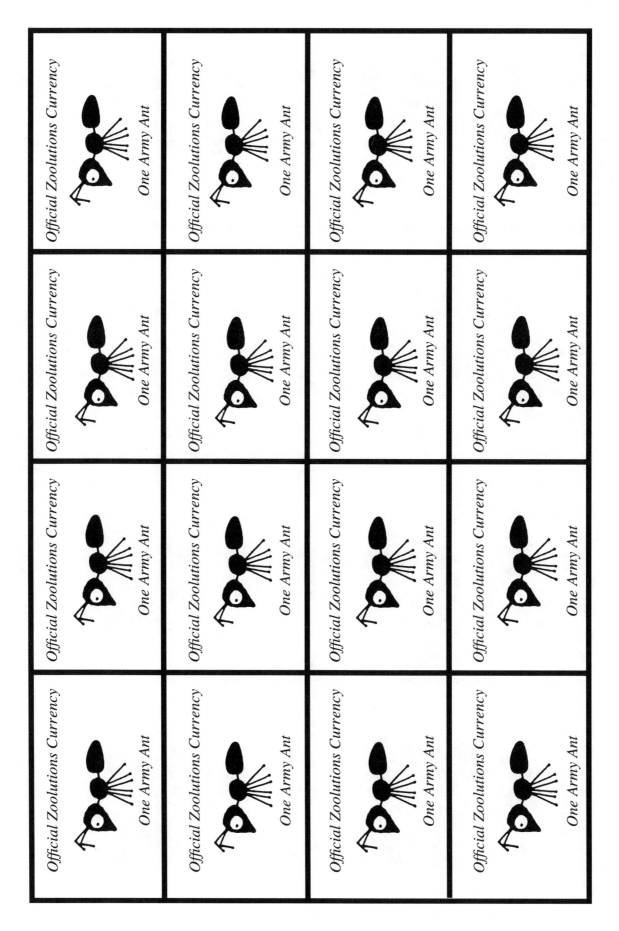

ABOUT THE AUTHORS

Anne Burgunder is a graduate of Duquesne University and the Bank Street College Math Leadership program. She is active in the math reform movement and serves on the Pennsylvania State Team for Math, Science, and Technology Reform. Anne has been developing units which integrate mathematics into the content areas and has presented these at local, regional, and national conferences. She currently teaches fourth grade in Pittsburgh and serves as a math consultant for her school as well as outside school districts.

Vaunda Nelson is a graduate of the Bread Loaf School of English and the University of Pittsburgh School of Library and Information Science. While she has devoted most of her working life to education and children, Vaunda is also the author of *Possibles* (1995), *Mayfield Crossing* (1993) and *Always Gramma* (1988) (G. P. Putnam's Sons) and has been a member of the John Newbery Award committee. Currently, she is Senior Librarian at the Rio Rancho Public Library, Rio Rancho, New Mexico.

Zoolutions received the 1994 Association for Library Service to Children/ Econo-Clad Literature Program Award given annually to a unique and outstanding program which promotes life-long reading.